Cogs in the Wheel

Contents

The Industrial Revolution	4
Before the Revolution	6
The Rise of the Machines	8
The Age of Steam	10
America Advances	12
The American System	14
The Canadian Problem	16
The Need for Speed	18
City Life	20
Child Labor	22
The Second Revolution	24
Going Global	28
Glossary	30
Index	31
Research Starters	32

Features

IN FOCUS
The Industrial Revolution began in Britain. Find out why Britain was ripe for development in **Why Britain?** on page 9.

PROFILE
One man invented the steam engine and gave his name to a unit of electricity. Turn to page 10 to learn more.

TIME LINK
The nineteenth century had its own version of the Internet. Read **Instant Communication** on page 15 to discover what it was.

FAST FACTS
How fast did people travel in the 1800s? Turn to page 18 to learn the answer.

SITESEEING · PAST & FUTURE
Who wrote about child labor?
Visit **www.rigbyinfoquest.com**
for more about **THE INDUSTRIAL REVOLUTION**.

The Industrial Revolution

Between the years of 1760 and 1850, the lives of millions of people in Britain, the United States, and parts of Europe underwent a series of dramatic changes. This was the period we call the Industrial Revolution. Revolutions often involve war or conflict, but the Industrial Revolution was a different kind of event. It was a revolution in technology, and the changes it brought about were the most significant since humans turned from hunting and gathering to farming.

In less than a century, enormous advances in transportation, communications, and manufacturing forever altered people's lives. People could now buy affordable manufactured goods and travel long distances cheaply and quickly. The changes that took place 200 years ago resulted in the way we live our lives today.

Transportation

Communications

Manufacturing

5

Before the Revolution

Before the Industrial Revolution, conditions for working people hadn't changed much for centuries. Most people worked on farms or made a variety of crafts. There were no machines, so the working day was often long and physically tough, leaving little time for leisure.

During the 1700s, significant changes took place in the British countryside. The population grew swiftly. At the same time, there were mass layoffs of farmworkers, many of whom headed for the cities in search of work.

Potters, wheelwrights, and coopers, or barrel makers, were common types of craftspeople in country towns and villages.

The Agricultural Revolution

Improvements in agriculture helped make the Industrial Revolution possible. New farming methods and tools, along with better animal care, enabled farmers to provide food, wool, and other raw materials for the newly industrialized cities.

Mechanization
New machinery brought increased efficiency, putting many farmworkers out of jobs.

Crop Rotation
More effective planting produced extra food for animals and restored nutrients to the soil.

Selective Breeding
Scientific breeding methods resulted in larger, healthier, and more productive stock.

Enclosure
Increased private ownership, or enclosure, of property forced many small farmers from their land.

The Rise of the Machines

Before the Industrial Revolution, **textiles** were made in cottages by artisans. Women and children spun the yarn, from which the men wove fabric on traditional hand looms. Six to eight spinners were needed to supply yarn for every weaver. Spinning on old-fashioned spinning wheels was an important part of many households' incomes.

The invention in Britain of the spinning jenny, which could do the work of dozens of hand spinners, put many women out of work and created widespread hardship. It was followed by powered looms, which did the same for many men. Those craftspeople who were able to find work in the new factories may have felt themselves to be little more than cogs in a giant wheel.

Spinning wheel

Weaving loom

Why Britain?

Britain was an ideal birthplace for the Industrial Revolution. It was rich in some raw materials such as coal and had access to others from its overseas colonies. It had several universities, and its government encouraged people to develop new inventions and methods of production.

The Spinning Jenny

Here is a picture of an early spinning jenny. It was invented by James Hargreaves, who some say named it after his daughter. Instead of spinning a single thread like the old-fashioned spinning wheel shown at left, the operator of the spinning jenny could spin eight threads at once by turning a single wheel. Later, the number of threads was increased to eighty or more, and the machines were powered by water or steam.

The Age of Steam

Two sources of power fueled the Industrial Revolution: coal and steam. Factories, ships, and trains were all steam powered. The furnaces that created the steam were fired with coal. Before, factories were powered by waterwheels so they had to be built beside rivers. With the arrival of steam engines, factories were increasingly located near coalfields. As a result, towns in those areas grew rapidly.

Coal was plentiful in Britain and had many uses. Metal workers discovered it could be used to speed up the production of iron and brass. Iron quickly replaced wood in much manufacturing and engineering.

Boiler

PROFILE

James Watt (1736-1819)

James Watt invented the first workable steam engine. Thanks to Watt, it was possible to make a steam engine strong enough to power huge iron machines.

At the age of 29, Watt designed a new type of steam engine that used only a quarter of the steam used by older versions. With a business partner, he developed steam engines for use in textile and flour mills. Today, Watt's name is still used as a measure of electrical energy: the watt.

Chimney

An Industrial Steam Engine

Water is heated in a boiler, making steam. The steam goes through a pipe to a cylinder, where it pushes a piston in and out. This turns a wheel, which is attached by a drive belt to a machine. The spinning drive belt makes the machine run.

Drive belt

Furnace

Cylinder and piston

Until the Industrial Revolution, most coal was taken from shallow pits or tunnels. The sudden demand for coal caused mine owners to search for new coal seams many hundreds of feet below ground. Thousands of men, women, and children were employed in the mines, risking death from accidents, poisonous gases, and the respiratory disease known as black lung.

America Advances

Much of the raw cotton for Britain's growing textile industry came from the southern states of the United States. In 1793, an American named Eli Whitney invented the cotton gin. This was a device for removing the seeds from cotton fiber, which previously had been done by hand. The cotton gin helped make cotton growing profitable, so that by the middle of the nineteenth century, the U.S. was producing 75% of the world's cotton. America's Industrial Revolution had begun.

Industrialization spread rapidly. The United States was part of a vast continent with abundant forests and natural resources. The government knew that it needed to develop industry quickly in order to protect its newly found independence. It encouraged people with knowledge and skills to emigrate to the New World.

Cotton gin

Having numerous rivers meant that water was American industry's main source of power for many years. Steam power arrived with the opening up of coal reserves in the 1820s. Soon, steamboats were carrying cotton for trade along the great southern U.S. rivers.

Isambard Kingdom Brunel

The United States not only provided the raw materials but also was the largest market for Britain's textile manufacturers. More and more sailing ships, called packets, crisscrossed the Atlantic, loaded with goods and passengers. A single crossing could take three or four weeks. For the brilliant young engineer Isambard Kingdom Brunel, that was too slow. Brunel built the first paddle steamer to cross the Atlantic. On her first trip, the *Great Western* reached New York from England in just 15 days.

The American System

While the use of machines had created a surplus of workers in Britain, the United States had the opposite problem. So many people were heading west to establish new territories that there was a shortage of labor. The solution was the rapid invention of machines that could replace skilled human labor.

In 1797, Eli Whitney, the inventor of the cotton gin, promised to supply the United States Army with 10,000 muskets in two years. Until then, guns had all been individually handmade by artisans. Whitney built a factory where unskilled workers could make gun parts from patterns. Although it took Whitney nearly eight years to deliver his order, by then he had developed the system of **mass production** using **interchangeable parts**, often called the American system of manufacturing.

The *Titanic*

America Advances continued

TIME LINK

Instant Communication

Dot-dot-dot dash-dash-dash dot-dot-dot! The distress signal sent out by the *Titanic* as she sank on April 14, 1912, was a product of the U.S. Industrial Revolution. It was in Morse code, a language devised in the 1830s by Samuel Morse for use with his new invention, the telegraph.

The telegraph enabled people to send and receive messages almost instantaneously. Like the Internet today, the telegraph rapidly caused people to become better informed because news and business information could now circle the globe in minutes instead of weeks.

Samuel Morse

Key for sending messages in Morse code

Above: The telegraph operator on the ship *SS Carpathia* was the first to hear the *Titanic*'s distress signal.

The Canadian Problem

In many parts of the world, the Industrial Revolution progressed slowly. Some powerful nations, such as France and Russia, were hindered by political unrest or sheer size. Only Germany's industrial output challenged that of Britain and the United States.

Canada, however, had a unique problem that only the technology of the Industrial Revolution could solve. The Great Lakes and the St. Lawrence River formed a vital route from the heart of the country to the Atlantic Ocean, 2,300 miles away. The problem was that there were many rapids along the way. Starting in the nineteenth century, the Canadians set out to build a complex system of waterways, canals, and **locks** that would enable ships to travel the entire distance.

The project was finally completed in 1959 with the opening of the St. Lawrence Seaway.

Above: A ship navigates a lock in the Welland Canal.

Left: Sailing ships on the St. Lawrence River

Getting Around the Falls

One of the biggest obstacles to water transportation in Canada was Niagara Falls. Between Lake Erie and Lake Ontario, the Niagara River plunges 100 yards, over some of the world's largest waterfalls. The solution was to build a canal that completely bypassed the river and the falls.

The Welland Canal opened in 1829. It has since been rebuilt three times to accommodate ever larger ships. It is regarded as one of the most important engineering projects begun during the Industrial Revolution.

The Need for Speed

For ordinary people, one of the most startling changes during the Industrial Revolution was the increased pace of life. New machines produced yarn and cloth many times faster than before. Steam-powered printing presses printed thousands of pages a day. Cities doubled and quadrupled in size.

The most important symbol of the new quest for speed was the railroad. Before trains, most overland journeys were made on horseback, in coaches, or on foot. Roads were poor and journeys often took several days. Large loads were transported along canals on horse-drawn barges. The first trains crawled along at four miles per hour, but before long, speeds of 60 miles per hour were possible. Travel times shrank from days to hours. Trains were safe and relatively affordable, making long-distance travel popular.

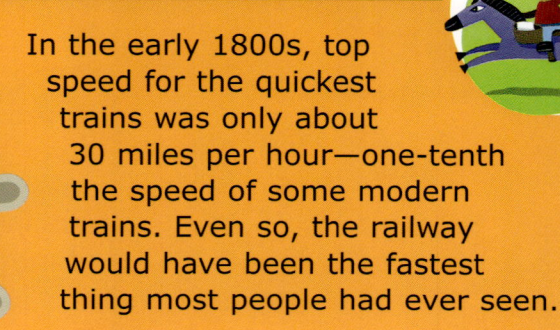

FAST FACTS

In the early 1800s, top speed for the quickest trains was only about 30 miles per hour—one-tenth the speed of some modern trains. Even so, the railway would have been the fastest thing most people had ever seen.

The Great Railroad Race

The locomotive had its greatest impact in the United States. In 1862, the building of a new railroad to connect the cities of the East with the new territories of California and Oregon in the West was announced. Work on the Pacific Railroad, as it was called, began at both ends. The project turned into a competition as the two companies involved raced to lay the most track. Progress was slow and dangerous. The workers, mainly Chinese and Irish immigrants, encountered mountains, blizzards, and frequent attacks by Native Americans who were angry at the loss of their land. The railroad was finally completed in 1869.

City Life

An important feature of the Industrial Revolution was the movement of people from the country to the cities. The lack of farmwork and a rising population meant that huge numbers of people were desperate for employment. Farm laborers and artisans began to flock to the rapidly growing cities.

The growth of cities in the eighteenth and nineteenth centuries was amazing. Cities that were near coalfields or seaports grew fastest. In England, Manchester grew five times bigger between 1700 and 1760. The population of Liverpool, a busy port, increased by ten times in the same period.

Cities in the United States

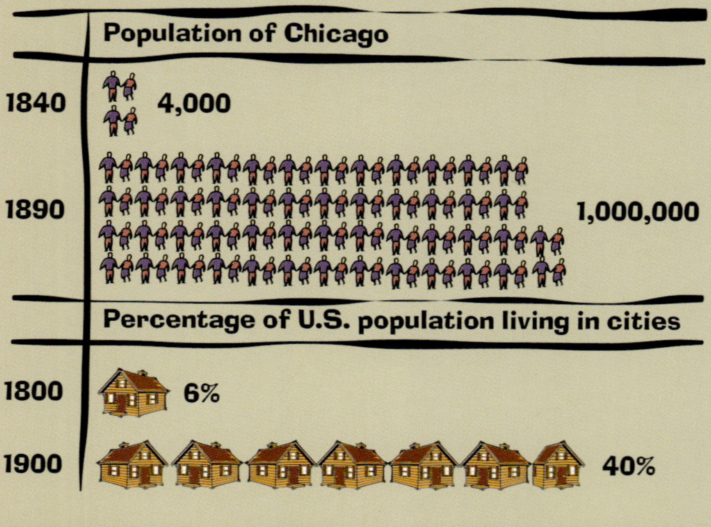

Population of Chicago

Year	Population
1840	4,000
1890	1,000,000

Percentage of U.S. population living in cities

Year	Percentage
1800	6%
1900	40%

Slumming It

If people thought the move to the cities was going to greatly improve their lives, they were in for a shock. Many found themselves living in cheap, back-to-back houses that were cold, damp, and without bathrooms or running water. Diseases such as cholera and typhus were a constant threat. Waste was simply dumped into the streets.

Above: The streets of this northern English factory town are black with soot from the distant chimneys.

Below: Children from the slums line up for the camera.

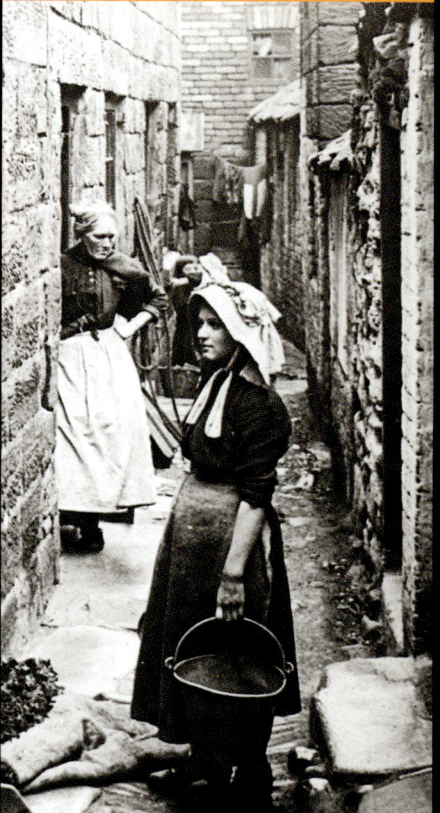

Child Labor

Life could be hard for children in the new industrial cities. There were few schools for the poor, and children as young as six were often sent to work in the textile mills. There they worked up to 14 hours a day for a fraction of the adult wage. Factory owners plucked children from orphanages to work. These unlucky children were called **pauper apprentices** and sometimes received only food and shelter for their hard work.

Working conditions were primitive and dangerous. In addition to accidents, the long hours spent standing could lead to crippling health problems. Factory owners severely punished children who were late to work or who they felt were not working hard enough.

This girl (left) is so young that she needs to stand on a box to work the machinery. The barefooted boys (right) are being supervised by older men.

City Life continued

PROFILE

To the Rescue

Not everyone was so cruel. Robert Owen (1771–1858) was a factory owner who built nurseries and schools for young children. He stopped employing children younger than ten, and the older youth he employed had to attend a specially-built high school every day.

Jane Addams (1860–1935) created Hull House in Chicago. This was a place where the poor could come to receive food, shelter, and an education. Addams helped establish new child labor laws that gave protection to children.

Robert Owen

Jane Addams

SITESEEING PAST & FUTURE

Who wrote about child labor?

Visit **www.rigbyinfoquest.com**
for more about **THE INDUSTRIAL REVOLUTION.**

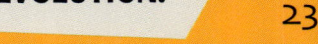

The Second Revolution

Although the Industrial Revolution eventually slowed down, a wave of new technology in the late nineteenth century brought about what is often called the Second Industrial Revolution. This time, the leaders were the United States, Germany, and France, and the advances were in electricity, chemicals, communications, and steel.

Developments in chemistry led to the invention of **synthetic** drugs, dyes, and textiles and to breakthroughs in the use of oil. Meanwhile, factories were growing larger, replacing steam-driven machines with more efficient electric engines. The invention of the electric lightbulb allowed factories to stay open longer, increasing productivity.

Oil Fever

Why would anyone pay $5,000 for that worthless piece of land? wondered the locals in Titusville, Pennsylvania, one day in 1854. The answer was they wanted its oil. New methods of refining oil had caused the value of oil to rise rapidly. The oil well built by Edwin Drake at Titusville in 1859 (left) was the first in the United States. Within 50 years, the U.S. produced more

PROFILE

Henry Ford and the Universal Car

In 1908, Henry Ford (1863–1947) mass-produced the first Model T Ford. Sturdy and dependable, it was an immediate success. In 1914, the first moving **assembly line** opened at the Ford factory in Michigan. Workers stood still while parts were brought to them on a conveyor belt, greatly reducing the assembly time.

Ford had a vision of an automobile that was affordable for everyone. He paid his workers twice the usual amount so that they could own a "Tin Lizzy," as the Model T was known. By 1926, half of all the world's cars were Model T Fords.

Henry Ford

Model T Ford

oil than the rest of the world combined. At first, oil was used mainly to make kerosene for lighting. Eventually, many other uses were found, including gasoline for cars, asphalt for roads, plastics, and makeup.

Some new developments in science had unexpected results. When Guglielmo Marconi **patented** wireless telegraphy in 1897, he saw it as a tool to send Morse code messages over long distances. By the 1920s, the radio, or "wireless," was the most popular form of entertainment, bringing music, drama, news, and comedy into millions of homes.

Photography was a product of recent chemical discoveries. When combined with the new technologies of the electric motor and the lightbulb, the result was motion pictures. Although the first films were basic, audiences in the late 1890s were astonished by the novelty of moving images on a screen.

FAST FACTS

In 1938, a realistic radio play about a Martian invasion of Earth caused widespread panic in the United States!

The Second Revolution continued

Alexander Graham Bell (1847-1922)

One of the most important inventions of the Second Industrial Revolution was the telephone. Although a number of people contributed to this invention, it was Alexander Graham Bell who finally achieved a successful design. When Bell started working on his "electrical speech machine" in 1874, most people wondered why anyone would want such a thing!

After two years of hard work, he made the first telephone call and said to his friend Thomas Watson, "Mr. Watson, come here. I want to see you."

Above: *The Great Train Robbery* (1903) was the first movie blockbuster.

Going Global

In some ways, the Industrial Revolution was really many revolutions, happening at different times in different parts of the world. Places such as Asia, India, and South America, that had provided raw materials for the first factories, had to wait many years to establish their own industries. Sometimes, as in China, the traditional ways worked so well that there seemed little reason to change.

In the twentieth century, the low pay rates for workers in less developed countries caused many large international companies to start building factories there. The dangers of industrialization, such as pollution and poor working conditions, have not changed much. The biggest challenge for the **developing countries** is to grow their industries, without repeating the mistakes of the industrialized nations.

These recent examples of transportation, communications, and manufacturing all come from Asia. How are they different from the ones shown on page 5?

Glossary

assembly line – a process by which a product is manufactured in stages by a line of workers

crop rotation – a system of planting fields with different crops each year to help control plant disease and improve the condition of the soil

developing country – a country that is moving from agriculture to industry

enclosure – the act of enclosing public land with fences to make it private property

industrialization – the development of industry

interchangeable part – a part that can be used in place of another

lock – a kind of gate used for holding water so boats can move from one level of a river or canal to another

mass production – the manufacture of an item in large numbers

mechanization – the introduction of machines in place of human labor

patent – a government license giving the sole right to make and sell a product for a certain time

pauper apprentice – a very poor person who is learning a trade or craft

selective breeding – breeding only from animals that have desirable characteristics

synthetic – made by combining chemicals

textile – any woven material

Index

Addams, Jane 23
agriculture 4, 6–7, 20
Bell, Alexander Graham 27
canals 16–18
child labor 22–23
cities 6–7, 18–23
coal 9–12, 20
communications 4–5, 15, 24, 26–27, 29
cotton 12
crafts 6, 8
electricity 10, 24, 26–27
Ford, Henry 25
mass production 14, 25
Morse, Samuel 15
oil 24–25
Owen, Robert 23
ships 10, 13, 15–17
spinning jenny 8–9
steam power 9–13, 18, 24
textiles 8–9, 12–13, 22, 24
trains 10, 18–19
Watt, James 10
Whitney, Eli 12, 14

Research Starters

1 Changes in farming helped the Industrial Revolution happen. Find out some ways farmers today are using new technology. How has science changed the food we eat?

2 Go back in time by researching your town's history. How big was your town in the nineteenth century? Where had the inhabitants come from, and what work did they do?

3 The telegraph brought about significant changes in communication. What new developments in communication have taken place in recent times? Describe the ways they have changed your life and the life of someone you know in the workforce.

4 Use the library or the Internet to research coal mining during the eighteenth and nineteenth centuries. Write a description of how life was for the mine workers.